Famous Myths and Legends of the World

Myths and Legends of:

AUSTRALIA, NEW ZEALAND, AND PACIFIC ISLANDS

WORLD
BOOK

a Scott Fetzer company
Chicago
www.worldbook.com

World Book, Inc.
180 North LaSalle Street
Suite 900
Chicago, Illinois 60601
USA

For information about other World Book publications, visit our website at **www.worldbook.com** or call **1-800-967-5325.**

Library of Congress Cataloging-in-Publication Data

Myths and legends of Australia, New Zealand, and Pacific islands.
    pages cm. -- (Famous myths and legends of the world)
   Summary: "Myths and legends from Australia, New Zealand, and Pacific Islands. Features include information about the history and culture behind the myths, pronunciations, lists of deities, word glossary, further information, and index"-- Provided by publisher.
    Includes index.
    ISBN 978-0-7166-2629-9
    1. Mythology, Aboriginal Australian--Juvenile literature.
    2. Aboriginal Australians--Folklore--Juvenile literature.
    3. Mythology, Māori--Juvenile literature. 4. Māori (New Zealand people)--Folklore--Juvenile literature. 5. Mythology, Polynesian--Juvenile literature. 6. Polynesians--Folklore--Juvenile literature. 7. Australia--Folklore--Juvenile literature.
    8. New Zealand--Folklore--Juvenile literature. 9. Islands of the Pacific--Folklore--Juvenile literature. I. World Book, Inc.
    II. Series: Famous myths and legends of the world.
    BL2600.M98 2015
    398.2099--dc23

                                2015014759

Set ISBN: 978-0-7166-2625-1
E-book ISBN: 978-0-7166-2641-1 (EPUB3)

Revised printing, 2016

Printed in China by PrintWORKS Global Services, Shenzhen, Guangdong
2nd printing May 2016

Writer: Anita Croy

Staff for World Book, Inc.
Executive Committee
President: Jim O'Rourke
Vice President and Editor in Chief: Paul A. Kobasa
Vice President, Finance: Donald D. Keller
Vice President, Marketing: Jean Lin
Director, International Sales: Kristin Norell
Director, Licensing Sales: Edward Field
Director, Human Resources: Bev Ecker

Editorial
Manager, Annuals/Series Nonfiction: Christine Sullivan
Managing Editor, Annuals/Series Nonfiction:
    Barbara Mayes
Administrative Assistant: Ethel Matthews
Manager, Indexing Services: David Pofelski
Manager, Contracts & Compliance
    (Rights & Permissions): Loranne K. Shields

Manufacturing/Production
Manufacturing Manager: Sandra Johnson
Production/Technology Manager: Anne Fritzinger
Proofreader: Nathalie Strassheim

Graphics and Design
Senior Art Director: Tom Evans
Coordinator, Design Development and Production:
    Brenda Tropinski
Senior Designers: Matthew Carrington,
    Isaiah W. Sheppard, Jr.
Media Researcher: Jeff Heimsath
Manager, Cartographic Services: Wayne K. Pichler
Senior Cartographer: John M. Rejba

Staff for Brown Bear Books Ltd
Managing Editor: Tim Cooke
Editorial Director: Lindsey Lowe
Children's Publisher: Anne O'Daly
Design Manager: Keith Davis
Designer: Kristine Hatch
Picture Manager: Sophie Mortimer

CONTENTS

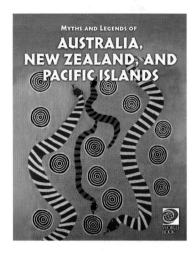

The Rainbow Snake is revered as a creator god. He was responsible for shaping the landscape, particularly the rivers. He also regenerates nature and helps human fertility.

Snake Dreaming (1989), acrylic on canvas by Billy Stockman Tjapaltjarri; Corbally Stourton Contemporary Art, Australia (Bridgeman Images)

Note to Readers:

Phonetic pronunciations have been inserted into the myths and legends in this volume to make reading the stories easier and to give the reader some of the flavor of the Australia, New Zealand, and Pacific Island cultures the stories represent. See page 64 for a pronunciation key.

The myths and legends retold in this volume are written in a creative way to provide an engaging reading experience and approximate the artistry of the originals. Many of these stories were not written down but were recited by storytellers from generation to generation. Even when some of the stories came to be written down, they likely did not feature phonetic pronunciations for challenging names and words! We hope the inclusion of this material will improve rather than distract from your experience of the stories.

Some of the figures mentioned in the myths and legends in this volume are described on page 60 in the section "Deities of Australia, New Zealand, and Pacific Islands." In addition, some unusual words in the text are defined in the Glossary on page 62.

INTRODUCTION

Since the earliest times, people have told stories to try to explain the world in which they lived. These stories are known as myths. Myths try to answer such questions as, How was the world created? Who were the first people? Where did the animals come from? Why does the sun rise and set? Why is the land devastated by storms or drought? Today, people often rely on science to answer many of these questions. But in earlier times—and in some parts of the world today—people explained natural events using stories about gods, goddesses, spirits of nature, and heroes.

Myths are different from folk tales and legends. Folk tales are fictional stories about animals or human beings. Most of these tales are not set in any particular time or place, and they begin and end in a certain way. For example,

The World of the Aboriginal People, page 10

many English folk tales begin with the phrase "Once upon a time" and end with "They lived happily ever after." Legends are set in the real world, in the present or the historical past. Legends distort the truth, but they are based on real people or events.

Myths, in contrast, typically tell of events that have taken place in the remote past. Unlike legends, myths have also played—and often continue to play—an important role in a society's religious life. Although legends may have religious themes, most are not religious in nature. The people of a society may tell folk tales and legends for amusement, without believing them. But they usually consider their myths sacred and completely true.

Most myths concern *divinities* (divine beings). These divinities have powers far greater than those of any human being. At the same time, however, many gods, goddesses, and heroes of mythology have human characteristics. They are guided by such emotions as love and jealousy, and they may experience birth and death. A number of mythological figures even look like human beings. In many cases, the human qualities of the divinities reflect a society's ideals. Good gods and goddesses have the qualities a society admires, and evil ones have the qualities it dislikes. In myths, the actions of these divinities influence the world of humans for better or for worse.

The World of Rapa Nui, page 58

Myths can sometimes seem very strange. They sometimes seem to take place in a world that is both like our world and unlike it. Time can go backward and forward, so it is sometimes difficult to tell in what order events happen. People may be dead and alive at the same time.

Myths were originally passed down from generation to generation by word of mouth. Partly for this reason, there are often different versions of the same story.

In early times, every society developed its own myths, though many myths across cultures share similar themes,

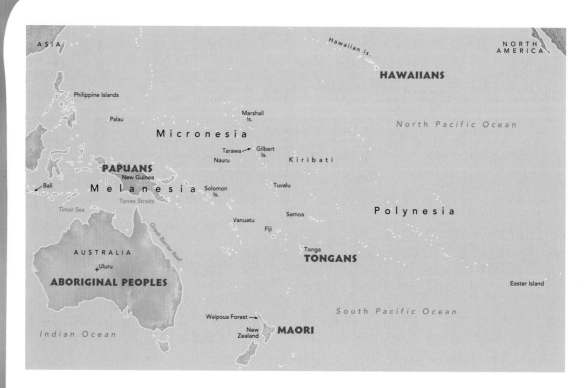

The peoples of Australia, New Zealand, and the islands of the Pacific Ocean originally came from Asia and spread throughout the region over thousands of years.

such as a battle between good and evil. The myths of a society generally reflect the landscape, climate, and society in which the storytellers lived.

Myths of Australia, New Zealand, and Pacific Islands

The island peoples of the central Pacific Ocean come from different traditions. The Aboriginal peoples of Australia lived in isolation from other peoples for many centuries before European settlers arrived in 1788. Their myths talk about the Dreamtime. This was a period when the ancestor spirits of the different Aboriginal bands created Earth as it is today. Their exploits are characterized by a close bond between the people and the natural landscape.

The Pacific Islands, which are often referred to as Oceania, are divided into three main groups: Polynesia, Melanesia, and Micronesia. The islands have a history of travel and cultural interchange. Polynesia is the easternmost group of islands and includes the large islands of Hawaii and New Zealand. Many mythical elements are shared throughout Polynesia. Melanesia is the central area, and is dominated by the island of Papua. The myths of the two areas are strikingly different from one another. Micronesia had a history of ancestor worship.

The World of the Māori, page 24

Today, Aboriginal peoples and Pacific Islanders still tell the old myths. The stories inform people about their distant history and why society is structured as it is. The myths show people how to behave in the world and find their way in it.

By studying myths, we can learn how different societies have answered basic questions about the world and the individual's place in it. We can learn how a people developed a particular social system with its many customs and ways of life. We can better understand the feelings and values that bind members of society into one group. We can compare the myths of various cultures to discover how these cultures differ and how they resemble one another. We also study myths to try to understand why people behave as they do.

MARMOO AND

For the Aboriginal people of Australia, this story helps to explain the creation of their world and why there are different kinds of birds and insects.

In the earliest Dreamtime, Baiame (by uh mee), the Creator Spirit, came down to Earth. There was nothing here, so Baiame decided to make a beautiful place to live. He put mountains in some places, made other places flat, and filled other places with sand. Finally, he created the seashores.

When he had finished, Baiame decided to add plants. In the sandy deserts, he put shrubs and wildflowers. He made ferns and trees to live in the mountains, and grasses and shrubs to live by the seashores. Next, he added water so that the plants could survive where he had placed them. He gave waterholes to the deserts, rivers to the plains, and cascading waterfalls to the mountains. Along the seashores, he created deep oceans and gentle seas. Then he added a breeze. He was so pleased with his creation that he decided to stay on Earth. He moved to the top of a mountain with Mother Nature.

Meanwhile, Baiame's enemy, the evil Marmoo (mahr moo), had been enviously watching. He complained to his wife. "If you think you can make a better Earth, why don't you?" she replied. "I have an even better idea," said Marmoo, "I will destroy everything Baiame has made."

Marmoo went into his cave and started to make insects. Some of them crawled, some flew, some burrowed, and some wriggled. He made millions of these tiny creatures and released them to attack Baiame's beautiful Earth. The insects

BAIAME

moved like a brown cloud across the land, killing any plants they came across.

From high upon the mountain, Baiame spotted the brown patch of insects, which seemed to be growing bigger and bigger. "What is happening?" he cried to Mother Nature. "Who would do such an awful thing?" she asked. Baiame wondered how they could stop the huge invasion of insects.

"I know what to do," said Mother Nature, disappearing into her cave. She came out carrying a creature she had made. It had long legs, a round body, and a sharp beak. The feathers on its tail were beautifully curved like the sides of a small harp. "What is it?" asked Baiame. "A bird, a lyrebird (LYR burd)," replied Mother Nature. "Just watch what it will do."

She released the bird, which flew off. Soon it was gobbling up insects as fast as it could. Mother Nature realized more birds were needed to stop the insects, so she called her Good Spirits to help her. They made all kinds of birds, from huge black swans to small finches and tiny wrens. Some of the birds were brightly colored, and others were dark.

As the birds were made, they flew from the cave and began to gobble up the insects. Soon there were just as many insects as were needed. Today, we have Marmoo to thank for the insects in the world and Mother Nature to thank for the birds.

World of THE ABORIGINAL PEOPLE

The Aboriginal (AB uh RIHJ uh nuhl) people of Australia are the first people of Australia. They are also called Aborigines (AB uh RIHJ uh neez). The ancestors of today's Aboriginal people arrived in Australia at least 50,000 years ago. By 30,000 to 25,000 years ago, they had colonized most of the country, from the tropical rain forests to the central deserts.

A painting by an Aboriginal artist depicts some native animals in the x-ray style, in which internal organs and bones are clearly visible.

DREAMTIME

The myths of the Aboriginal people of Australia have their roots in the Dreamtime or Creation Time, when only the ancestors existed. The Dreamtime refers to both a period of time and a form of existence, or being. In time, it refers to that early period when supernatural ancestors (who often took the form of animals) traveled across Australia shaping its landscape. As a state of being, Dreamtime refers to the rituals people perform or visits they make to places thought to be *sacred* (holy) to keep alive the idea of the Dreamtime. Rituals include movements, sayings, music, and foods—sometimes connected to special places—that follow and stand for certain ideas and beliefs.

Kata Tjuta (kah tah choo tah), a rock formation consisting of 36 sandstone domes, is a major landmark in Uluru-Kata Tjuta National Park in Australia's Northern Territories. Kata Tjuta is sacred to the Anangu people, an Australian Aboriginal group who have lived in the area for more than 22,000 years and help manage the site. The park includes the giant outcrop of rock known as Uluru, which is also spiritually significant to the Anangu people.

ABORIGINAL MYTHS

Stories of the Aboriginal people of Australia have traditionally been passed down by word of mouth and were not written down. As a result, there is no single version of any myth. Aboriginal myths are usually told in song cycles, which may run to hundreds of verses. The length and complexity of any version of a myth depends on the circumstances under which it is told and the audience for which it is performed. Some myths are heard only by the elders in the community.

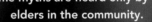

An Aboriginal elder shows young men how to throw a hunting spear. Many Aborigines still follow the traditional practices of their ancestors.

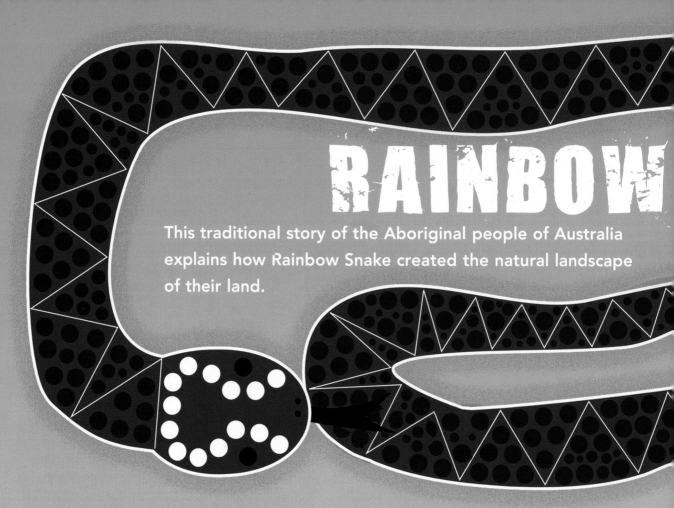

RAINBOW

This traditional story of the Aboriginal people of Australia explains how Rainbow Snake created the natural landscape of their land.

Kunmanggur (koon mahng gur), the Rainbow Snake, was the father of Tjinimin (chihn ihm ihn), the Bat, and the sisters called the Green Parrot Women. One day, the sisters set off to search for food. Tjinimin followed, planning to chase and torment his sisters. He soon caught up with the Green Parrot Women and attacked them. But they escaped and determined they would get their revenge upon Tjinimin.

The next day, the Green Parrot Women hurried to cross a river before Tjinimin could get there. When Tjinimin got to the river, the women called upon a swarm of hornets to attack him. The hornets stung Tjinimin all over his body. As he stumbled into the river, the current caught him and carried him out to sea. But Tjinimin was not defeated; he managed to swim back to dry land, coming ashore at the rocky base of a cliff.

As Tjinimin rested, he saw the fire of the Green Parrot Women at the top of the cliff and called out for help. The women agreed to throw down a rope and pull him up. Tjinimin began to climb. But just as he reached the cliff top, the women

SNAKE

to a big ceremony. The famous songman, the Diver Bird, came. Kunmanggur played a wind instrument called a didgeridoo (DIHJ uhr uh DOO), while Tjinimin led the dancing. During one dance, Tjinimin grabbed a spear and stabbed his father again and again. In an instant, all the dancers turned into flying foxes and birds and flew away, crying. Tjinimin fled.

Kunmanggur slithered away, trying to stop the bleeding from the wounds Tjinimin had given him. Everywhere his blood fell on the ground, water gushed forth. In one place, he left the shape of his body and other marks on a rock wall. In another place, he left his possessions—his stone axe, fishing net, and forehead band.

cut the rope. Crashing to the rocks below, he was smashed to pieces. But even that was not the end of Tjinimin. He sang magic songs, and soon his body had healed. To test that he really did possess magic powers, he cut off his nose and then restored it through his magic songs.

Pleased with his strength and magic powers, Tjinimin decided that he would kill his father. Kunmanggur, the Rainbow Snake, realized that his son was plotting against him, but he did not do anything to prevent it. Tjinimin returned to his father's camp and invited everyone

Finally, Kunmanggur, the Rainbow Snake, came to the sea. As he slipped into the water, he gathered up all the fire in the world and put it on his head as a headdress. Those watching tried to snatch the last flame before he disappeared under the waves, but it was too late. All the fire had gone out. Much later, Pilirin, the Kestrel, the god of fire, returned fire to the people by rubbing two sticks together to create sparks.

The World of THE OUTBACK

Many of the Aboriginal people of Australia live in the outback, the rugged rural interior of the continent. The landscape of the outback consists mainly of deserts, dry grasslands, and weathered and eroded mountains.

The Rainbow Snake (below) is one of the most important figures in Aboriginal art. The Rainbow Snake is revered as a creator god. He was responsible for shaping the landscape, particularly the rivers, and he produced spirit children. His most important feature is that he *regenerates* nature (brings nature back to life) and helps human fertility.

Burrunggui (Nourlangie Rock) in the Northern Territory's Kakadu National Park (above) displays many examples of Aboriginal rock paintings in its shelters. Aboriginal people believe ancestral beings, called Dreamings, traveled across the land, making and naming the places and people who would belong there. These ancestral beings never died but merged with the natural world. Some of the Dreamings went into the sky or into the ground, or merged into hills, rocks, or water holes. Others became plants, animals, and people.

ABORIGINAL PEOPLE

The ancestors of the Aboriginal people of Australia most likely settled on that continent at least 50,000 years ago. The earliest settlers probably arrived from East Asia during the last Ice Age, when sea levels were much lower and a land bridge joined Indonesia and Australia. They probably traveled along the coasts, where they could hunt and collect food. There may have been as many as 500 Aboriginal tribes at one time, speaking as many as 200 different languages and many hundreds of dialects.

Many Aboriginal artists still paint in traditional styles. Sometimes the pictures of animals are like x-ray images, where the bones can be seen through the skin. The artists often create pictures from many dots. The colors of the dots are related to the Australian landscape: the yellow of the sun, the red of the desert, the brown of the earth, and the white of the clouds. The pictures often show Australian animals or stories from the Dreamtime.

The eucalyptus (YOO kuh LIHP tuhs) is one of the most common trees in Australia. In the outback, the tree grows mostly along streams. Aboriginal people used eucalyptus bark to make containers to carry food and water and eucalyptus leaves to make medicines.

Alinga and the Creation of Uluru

The Aboriginal peoples of Australia told this myth to explain one of the world's most famous geographical features—the huge, red rock that rises from the flat lands at the center of the Australian continent.

A long time ago, at the beginning of time, there lived Alinga (uh leen guh), the Lizard Man. He was a powerful warrior who was respected by everyone across the land. His favorite weapon was his giant boomerang, which possessed special powers. He could throw the boomerang great distances. In fact, Alinga was so big and his boomerang so magical that when Alinga threw the weapon, it would sometimes take weeks or even months to come back. When the boomerang disappeared for long periods, however, Alinga did not worry. He was a patient man, and he knew that eventually his boomerang would return.

One day, Alinga took his boomerang out of his possum-skin belt. He decided to throw the boomerang farther than he had ever thrown it before. He wanted to see how far it would go and how long he would have to wait for it to return. He pulled his arm a long way back, tensed his muscles, and then launched the boomerang with great force.

This time, the boomerang was not gone for just weeks or even months. No, the weeks and months stretched into years, and still the boomerang did not return.

Eventually, Alinga could wait no longer. Although he had other boomerangs, the missing boomerang was special to him. Finally, he set off on a journey to find his beloved weapon.

Alinga walked and walked. He walked across vast stretches of open desert, but there was no sign of his boomerang. He walked to the lands far to the north, but still there was no sign of his boomerang. During his search, he created many parts of the landscape. For example, when he felt cold at night, he would make a campfire. Today, coal can be found at these places. When Alinga was attacked by monsters, he killed them. The monsters' bodies still lie as boulders on the watery beds of billabongs.

After searching fruitlessly for the boomerang, Alinga turned south. He traveled for weeks across the harshest country he had ever seen. Then one day, Alinga finally found his boomerang.

The boomerang was stuck hard into the ground. So much time had passed and there had been so many sandstorms that the boomerang had turned into a giant red rock. Alinga grabbed the rock and tried to lift it. As he struggled, his fingers carved gulleys and caves in the rock. But the rock was too heavy to be moved, even by such a strong warrior. Finally, Alinga gave up and decided to settle down near the boomerang.

This enormous rock was right in the middle of Australia, and the Aboriginal people called it Uluru. All the lizards that live in the caves at the foot of the rock are the descendants of Alinga, the Lizard Man.

The World of ULURU

Uluru is a giant outcrop of rock in the Northern Territory of Australia. It rises abruptly 1,100 feet (335 meters) from the sand dune plains. The name *Uluru* means *meeting place.* The rock measures 5 miles (8 kilometers) around its base.

Uluru is surrounded by the territory of the Anangu people, who consider it a sacred site. They care for the rock and guide visitors around it. Although it is permitted to climb on the rock, the Anangu prefer that people not do so as a sign of respect for it. The Anangu believe that certain sites around Uluru are sacred also and need to be preserved. Visitors are not allowed to photograph these sites.

← An Aboriginal rock painting at the Ipolera Aboriginal Community in the Northern Territory shows images of the Dreamtime, also called the Dreaming. Stories of the Dreaming form the foundation of traditional Aboriginal society.

SACRED ULURU

Uluru is sacred to the Aboriginal people. They tell many myths about how the rock was created. According to one of these stories, Uluru was shaped and scarred by two serpent-shaped Dreamings who fought each other there. The appearance of Uluru can change. It can glow a bright red or, after a rain, appear silvery-gray.

↑

An Aboriginal musician plays a didgeridoo, an instrument made from a hollowed-out piece of wood. The Aborigines blow into these wooden pipes to produce a rhythmic, booming sound.

The ancestors of the Aboriginal peoples first used boomerangs more than 10,000 years ago. The sticks are shaped so that they spin as they fly, which steers them on a circular path. The boomerang "returns" to the thrower. Boomerangs are still used for hunting, either to try to hit birds and small game animals or to scare them out of hiding so that they can be caught. Today, boomerangs are usually associated with Australia, but in the past, they were also used in other cultures. The ancient Egyptian King Tutankhamun was buried with a number of boomerangs.

SONGLINES

According to Aboriginal beliefs, ancestral beings called Dreamings traveled across the land, making and naming the places, animals, plants, and people who would belong there. The Dreamings then merged with the natural world. "Songline" is an Aboriginal name for the routes the Dreamings followed. These tracks crossed great distances. When people perform Dreaming ceremonies, they try to bring together people from tribes along a songline.

EARTH AND SKY

The Māori of New Zealand have traditionally used this myth to explain the creation of the universe and such natural phenomena as the rain and wind. The myth also explains the importance of the god Tāne.

Long, long ago there was nothing—no ocean, no land, no sky. Everything was dark and shapeless, and only the gods existed. The Sky Father was the god Rangi (RAHN gee); his wife, Papa (pah pah), was the Earth Mother. They loved each other very much and always clung to each other as tightly as they could. They had 70 sons, each of whom was a god. The 70 sons lived with their mother and father in an extremely small space. They had hardly any room to move, and there was no light to see by.

"If only our parents weren't so close together," one of the sons grumbled. "Then we could have some light and room to move." Another of the sons suggested that they should separate Rangi and Papa. One after another, the sons tried to pull their parents apart. But it was impossible, no matter how hard the sons tried.

Finally, Tāne (TUH neh), the god of nature, took his turn. He lay on his back and began pushing Rangi's body with his feet. He pushed and pushed. Slowly but surely, Rangi inched away from Papa until, suddenly, Rangi's body flew so far away that the sons feared he would never stop. At once, the world was filled with a brilliant light. The sons were all pleased, except for Tāwhiri (tah HWEE ree), the

god of wind, who loved his father more than his mother. He flew up to the sky to be with Rangi.

Rangi was devastated at being parted from Papa, and he cried and cried. His tears fell as rain on Earth. Papa sighed and her breath became clouds in the sky. Tāne felt sorry for his parents. To help his mother overcome her loneliness, he covered her in forests and grass, which Rangi's tears watered. Tāne also filled the forests with colorful birds, whose singing enchanted Papa. "Papa is so beautiful," sighed Rangi to Tāne, "What will you do for me?" So Tāne flew to Rangi and gave him a golden sun to wear on the front of his blue robes. To make his father look even more magnificent by day, Tāne covered Rangi with a red cloak. Although the cloak has since slipped off, you can sometimes catch glimpses of its redness as the sun rises and sets. For night, Tāne gave Rangi the moon and the stars to keep the sky bright.

"Now there is only one thing missing," said Tāne. "We need people to live on Earth, to enjoy the forests and the birds and to sail on the waters." So Tāne made the first woman from the red earth of Papa. He breathed life into her and took her as his wife. Soon there were men and women all over Earth enjoying the many things that Tāne had created.

The World of
THE MĀORI

The Māori (MOW ree) are a Polynesian people of New Zealand. They were the first people to live in what is now that country. Today, they make up about 15 percent of New Zealand's population. Most scholars believe Māori first settled New Zealand around A.D. 1200. According to Māori tradition, however, they began arriving more than 1,800 years ago.

Tāne Mahuta (TUH neh mah oo tah) is a giant kauri (KOW ree) tree in ➡ the Waipoua (wai POO a) Forest on the North Island of New Zealand. The tree is about 170 feet (51.2 meters) tall and may be up to 2,500 years old. Its name honors Tāne, the god of nature who created the forests. The tree is the largest surviving example of the kauri trees that grew in the ancient subtropical rain forest that once covered large parts of New Zealand.

A Māori man sticks out his tongue during a haka, a native dance performed with traditional actions or poses, often accompanied by song. The haka was usually performed by Māori warriors before battle. Today it is often performed during welcome ceremonies or before New Zealand sports events. Māori tattoos, called moko, mark the man's face. Māori tattoos may indicate different stages of life, including becoming an adult. The designs help indicate a person's age and social position.

A carved wooden Māori mask shows the fierce face of a warrior. Such masks were intended to cause fear among the wearer's enemies.

THE MĀORI

The Māori are Polynesians. Historians think that the early Polynesians migrated from Southeast Asia, possibly from what is now the island of Taiwan. They know that western Polynesia was settled around 3,000 years ago, though the time of the settlement of eastern Polynesia is unclear. Studies of genetic material from Polynesians are giving scientists a better understanding of how this complex society evolved on a series of remote islands in the Pacific Ocean.

The Māori chief Tāmati Wāka Nene (1780?-1871) poses with his war club, in a painting from 1890. Māori chiefs led warriors into war, but they were also responsible for keeping social order and making sure the community had enough food.

The WAR GOD
Tūmatauenga

This traditional story explains the persistence of violence and warfare among the Māori and Polynesians.

Tāwhiri (tah HWEE ree), the god of winds and storms, was furious with his brothers, especially Tāne (TUH neh), the god of nature, for violently separating his parents, Rangi (RAHN gee), the Sky Father, and Papa, the Earth Mother. So Tāwhiri rushed down to Earth and began to fight with his brothers. Tāne and Tangaroa (tuhng uh RAW uh), the god of the sea, tried to hold Tāwhiri back, but they were no match for the god of winds, who unleashed the power of his stormy breath on the land and water.

Tūmatauenga (too mah tah oo EHN gah), the god of war, also joined the battle against Tāwhiri. Seeing that Tūmatauenga was willing to take on Tāwhiri, Tāne and Tangaroa fled, leaving Tūmatauenga alone to face Tāwhiri's anger. Being the god of war, Tūmatauenga quickly defeated Tāwhiri, making the wind die down and the seas become calm. But Tūmatauenga was so angry with his brothers for abandoning him in battle that he decided to take his revenge on them.

Tūmatauenga first decided he would destroy the good work of his brother Tāne, the god of nature. So Tūmatauenga made snares to trap the songbirds Tāne had put in the forests. Then Tūmatauenga made nets from flax plants so that he could ensnare the children of Tangaroa, the sea god. But Tūmatauenga did not stop there. He also turned on his other brothers. He pulled up the children of his brothers Haumia (huh oo mee uh), the god of wild food, and Rongo (raw ngaw), the god of cultivated food, by their hair (which was actually leaves) and left them in the sun to dry. Then he ate them.

Despite their cowardly behavior in the battle with Tāwhiri, Tūmatauenga's brothers were not easily overcome, and they refused to surrender. So Tūmata-

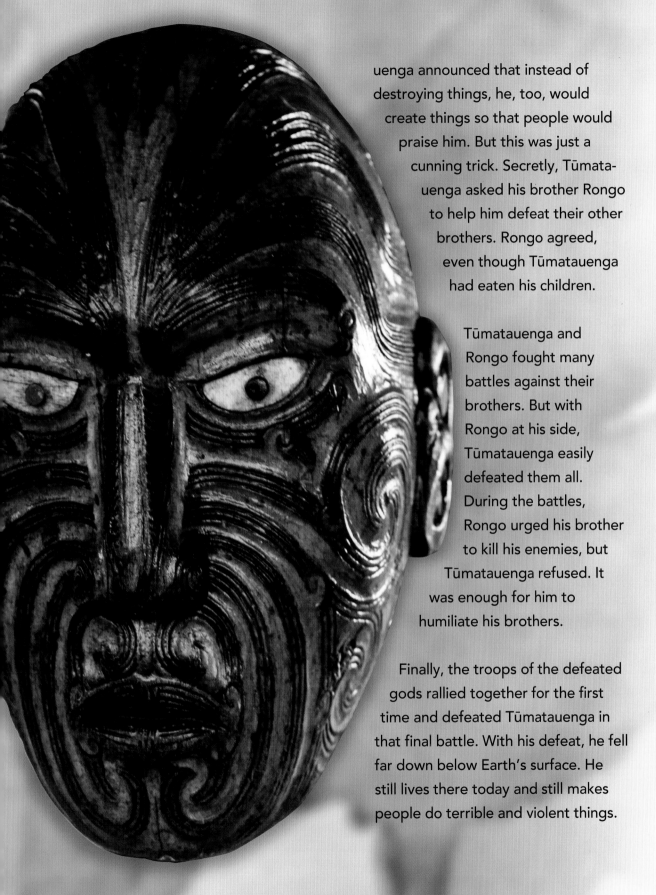

uenga announced that instead of destroying things, he, too, would create things so that people would praise him. But this was just a cunning trick. Secretly, Tūmata-uenga asked his brother Rongo to help him defeat their other brothers. Rongo agreed, even though Tūmatauenga had eaten his children.

Tūmatauenga and Rongo fought many battles against their brothers. But with Rongo at his side, Tūmatauenga easily defeated them all. During the battles, Rongo urged his brother to kill his enemies, but Tūmatauenga refused. It was enough for him to humiliate his brothers.

Finally, the troops of the defeated gods rallied together for the first time and defeated Tūmatauenga in that final battle. With his defeat, he fell far down below Earth's surface. He still lives there today and still makes people do terrible and violent things.

War was common in Polynesia. Wars were fought mainly to capture victims for human sacrifice and to seize farmland from neighboring chiefdoms. By killing his enemies, a chief could take their *mana* (power). Success in battle was also a way for commoners to increase their status.

New Zealand Māori (MOW ree) perform a haka, or traditional war dance. Māori warriors performed ritual dances before battle to try to scare off their opponents.

Young men from the Cook Islands, in the South Pacific Ocean, use spears to catch fish. Spears were also an important weapon in Polynesian battles.

POLYNESIA

Polynesia is the name of a group of widely scattered islands and archipelagos in the Pacific Ocean. Polynesia covers a roughly triangular area whose corners include Hawaii in the north, New Zealand in the south, and Easter Island (Rapa Nui [RAH puh NOO ee]) in the east. The name *Polynesia* comes from Greek words meaning *many islands*. The Polynesians are an Austronesian (AWS troh NEE zhuhn) people. The first Austronesians are thought to have lived on the island of Taiwan, off the coast of China.

Fields of taro, whose starchy stems are eaten as food across Polynesia, cover much of the Keanae Peninsula on the Hawaiian island of Maui. Many Polynesian peoples were expert farmers. But droughts and famine as well as territorial conflicts led to war. Polynesians' small islands soon became overcrowded, and war became a way of acquiring new land.

Māori in a traditional *waka* (canoe) enter the harbor at Auckland, New Zealand, during the opening ceremonies of a rugby competition. The Māori traditionally used canoes to travel to other islands to raid or fight. Such canoes usually featured elaborate carvings on each end. But the carvings could not be replicas of people because people were seen as the work of the gods, and it was an insult to the gods to imitate them. Instead, the features of the carvings were changed in certain ways so they could not be mistaken for people.

MAUI STEALS FIRE

This traditional Hawaiian story explains the dangers of fire, which was important on an island with active volcanoes.

Long ago, all the fire on Earth came from Mahuika (muh hoo ee kuh), the fire goddess. She was also the grandmother of the trickster Maui (MOW ee). One day, when he was bored, Maui decided that he would put out all the fires in the world. He wanted to see what would happen without fire's light and warmth.

So during the night, while everyone was asleep, Maui put out all fires everywhere. The next morning, as people woke up, they were shocked to find their fire pits dark and cold. "How will we prepare breakfast?" they asked. Nobody could cook or heat water. The villagers gathered to discuss what they should do next.

When Maui's mother realized that there was no fire, she called her servants and told them to go to Mahuika and ask for some fire. But the fire goddess was quite scary, so the servants refused. When Maui heard that his mother wanted someone to collect fire from his grandmother, he volunteered.

His mother explained to her son how to find the fire goddess's house. "I want you to be polite to your grandmother. And do not, under any circumstances, play any of your tricks on her," warned his mother. "You must show her respect because she is both your grandmother and the goddess of fire."

Maui set off from the village and, after a long journey, he finally reached his grandmother's house. It took him some time before he plucked up the courage to knock on her door and speak to her.

"I have come here to ask you to restore fire to all the villages," Maui said to Mahuika. Before she would do anything, however, the fire goddess wanted to know all about Maui: Who was he and where had he come from? He told her he was her grandson. "Do you come from the place where the wind begins?" she asked him. When he replied that he did, she replied, "Yes, you are my grandchild."

Mahuika agreed to give Maui fire. She did this by pulling out one of her fingernails and giving it to him. Fire flowed from the nail. Maui took it, thanked his grandmother, and left to make the long journey home. He had not gone very far, however, when the fire went out. So he turned back and asked his grandmother for another fingernail. She gave it to him, and he set off again. But before long, Maui was back at the fire goddess's, telling her that

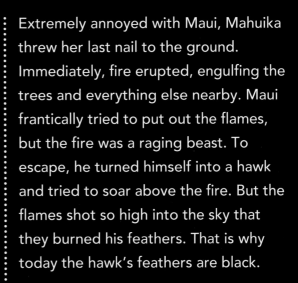

he needed another nail because the fire had gone from the second nail. Mahuika removed a third nail and gave it to her grandson. But exactly the same thing happened again. Eventually, Maui took all of Mahuika's fingernails and nearly all of her toenails. Finally, Mahuika realized that Maui was tricking her—he wanted to see what would happen when Mahuika had no fingernails or toenails left. And he had almost succeeded.

Extremely annoyed with Maui, Mahuika threw her last nail to the ground. Immediately, fire erupted, engulfing the trees and everything else nearby. Maui frantically tried to put out the flames, but the fire was a raging beast. To escape, he turned himself into a hawk and tried to soar above the fire. But the flames shot so high into the sky that they burned his feathers. That is why today the hawk's feathers are black.

Desperate for help, Maui called on his ancestor Tawhiri-matea (tah HWEE ree mah teh ah) and asked him to send rain. Soon big clouds had formed, and the rain began to fall in torrents. Before long, the water level had risen so high that only Mahuika's head remained above the flood; the deluge robbed her of all her special fires.

Once the fire was out, Maui made the long journey home to his village. When his parents saw his burns, they soon worked out what had happened and guessed Maui had been up to his usual tricks. They spoke angrily to him, but Maui was not sorry. He refused to acknowledge how close he had come to destroying the world with fire and how dangerous fire could be.

The World of THE HAWAIIANS

Polynesians were the first people to live in what is now Hawaii. They arrived in the Hawaiian island chain from other Pacific islands about 1,500 years ago. Another Polynesian people moved to Hawaii from Tahiti about A.D. 1200. This group won control over the earlier settlers.

Lava erupts from the *caldera* (crater) of Kilauea (KEE low AY ah), an active volcano on the island of Hawaii. Kilauea lies on the eastern slope of a larger volcano, Mauna Loa (MOW nuh LOH uh). The Hawaiian Islands were formed by volcanoes built up from the ocean floor.

MAUI

Maui (MOW ee) is the most famous and popular of all the Hawaiian gods, and his fame and popularity spread across Polynesia. He is considered a hero who does good, even though he can also misbehave, as he does in "Maui Steals Fire." One of the Hawaiian Islands is even named after him.

Fire dancing is common to many Polynesian cultures. Hawaiian dancers use twirling fire sticks to create spectacular effects.

34

A stream rushes through Iao Valley on the island of Maui. The volcanic islands of Hawaii are mostly rugged and rocky. In the valleys and on the coastal plains, however, the rich volcanic soil supports areas of thick tropical vegetation. This vegetation, in turn, supports a wide range of animal and bird life.

This *ki'i* (carved statues) is one of many that surround Hale o Keawe, the former burial place of 23 Hawaiian chiefs in Pu'uhonua o Honaunau National Historical Park. The park is considered a sacred site by many Hawaiians.

PELE'S ANGER

The Hawaiians tell this story to explain the origins of the volcanoes whose eruptions have occurred regularly on the islands.

arrived at what is now the island of Hawaii and burrowed into the Kilauea volcano. Happily, no water rushed in, so she decided this would be her new home.

One night, Pele fell into a deep, deep sleep—a trance. Her spirit left her body and followed the sound of music that was coming from the next island. When she arrived, her spirit took the form of a beautiful woman. The chief of the island, Lohiau (loh HEE ow), took one look at

The goddess Pele (PEH leh) decided to leave the Pacific island of Tahiti for a new home. Accompanied by many other gods, she traveled east, moving from island to island. At each new island, she dug a hole to create a place to live. But each time, seawater rushed into the hole and pushed her out. Eventually, Pele

her and fell deeply in love. After they spent three days together, Pele told Lohiau that she must leave, but she would send for him to join her on Hawaii.

Once Pele's spirit returned home and awakened her body, Pele called for her sister, Hi'iaka (hee ee ah kah). She asked Hi'iaka to travel to the neighboring island to collect Lohiau and gave Hi'iaka special powers. Pele told Hi'iaka that she must return within 40 days.

But Hi'iaka's journey proved to be difficult, and she had to use her special powers to overcome many hazards. The journey to Lohiau's island ended up taking many years. When Hi'iaka finally arrived, she discovered that the chief had died of a broken heart. But by using her special powers, Hi'iaka brought Lohiau back to life, and the two set off to meet Pele.

Pele, meanwhile, wondered why her sister was taking so long to bring Lohiau back to her. She grew extremely jealous and angry and, in her anger, she spit out lava streams that burned and destroyed everything in their path.

During their journey, Lohiau fell in love with Hi'iaka. But Hi'iaka was a loyal sister and refused Lohiau, knowing that Pele was waiting for him. When she finally delivered Lohiau to Pele, Hi'iaka was shocked to discover that everything on the island was shrivelled and blackened. She was so upset that she threw herself into Lohiau's arms. Seeing them, Pele erupted with fury, shooting out flames over the lovers. Lohiau was killed in the fire, but Hi'iaku was protected by her magic powers.

Once the flames had died down, Hi'iaka brought Lohiau back to life, and they fled Pele's island as fast as they could. Since that day, the jealous Pele has been alone. And whenever she thinks of how Lohiau and her sister betrayed her, she spits out rivers of hot, molten lava.

The World of PELE

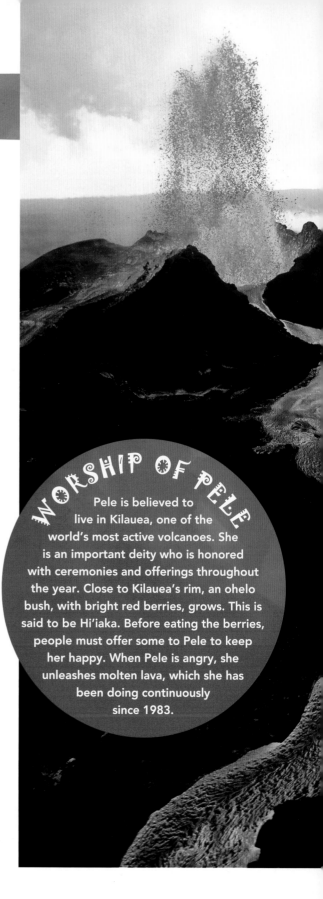

Lava flows from Puu Oo (poo oh oh), the easternmost of the *vents* (openings) of the Kilauea volcano on the island of Hawaii. The Hawaiian Islands are made up of eight large and more than 100 smaller volcanic islands. Hawaii's volcanoes are all shield volcanoes, mountains with broad, gently sloping sides that form gradually over time. The most recent island to appear is the Big Island of Hawaii, but a new island is slowly forming just 30 miles (48 kilometers) away.

WORSHIP OF PELE

Pele is believed to live in Kilauea, one of the world's most active volcanoes. She is an important deity who is honored with ceremonies and offerings throughout the year. Close to Kilauea's rim, an ohelo bush, with bright red berries, grows. This is said to be Hi'iaka. Before eating the berries, people must offer some to Pele to keep her happy. When Pele is angry, she unleashes molten lava, which she has been doing continuously since 1983.

Young girls perform the hula, the traditional dance of the first people on the Hawaiian Islands. According to one myth, the hula was first danced by Hi'iaka (hee ee ah kah) in order to calm her sister Pele (PEH leh) when the volcano goddess was angry. Today, the dance is accompanied by chanting and is a way to tell stories and preserve the Hawaiians' history and culture.

In Hawaii, the pu (POO) or conch shell is a traditional means of communication. The pu was blown to send messages between canoes at sea or between canoes and the land. Many Hawaiians see the pu as a divine gift from the ocean and often use it during religious ceremonies.

A Hawaiian double-hulled canoe is built for sailing long distances. The ancient Hawaiians were expert sailors. They navigated across the vast Pacific by using the positions of the sun, moon, and stars as a guide. These celestial bodies feature in many Hawaiian myths. Sailors also learned to recognize patterns of the wind and waves and studied the flight of birds to find their way from island to island.

Na Areau, the SPIDER GOD

The first people of the Gilbert Islands in the South Pacific Ocean told this myth to describe the creation of Earth, particularly the islands of Samoa and Tarawa.

At the beginning of time, there was nothing in the Darkness of Heaven and the Cleaving Together of Earth except one being. Where he came from and who his parents were, we do not know. He was called Na Areau te Moa-ni-bai (Sir Spider, the First-of-Things). He walked over heaven, which was like a hard rock stuck to Earth. He walked all alone, tapping the rock with his fingers. It sounded hollow. So he entered the rock and decided that people must be born beneath its shell.

He ordered the Sand to lie with the Water and make children, which were Na Atibu (nah ah tee boo), the first man, and Nei Teakea (neh ee teh ah keh ah),

the first woman. Na Atibu and Nei Teakea had many children, of which the last was called Na Areau the Younger. After a time, Na Areau te Moa-ni-bai decided his work was done, and he told Na Atibu to make a world of people while he went back to heaven. Na Atibu called his son Na Areau the Younger and told him what his grandfather had ordered.

So Na Areau the Younger searched for the many children of Na Atibu and Nei Teakea. He found them lying still as though they were dead. He stretched out his hand and touched them. One by one, they came to life, but when they got up they hit their heads on heaven,

which was still attached to Earth. Na Areau the Younger then called to his brother Riiki (ree ee kee), the great Eel, who walked on many legs. Na Areau the Younger said, "Sir, you are long and firm; could you lift heaven on your nose?" Eel coiled himself beneath heaven and pushed up. "Push harder," cried Na Areau, but heaven still clung to Earth. Na Areau asked his brothers Octopus, Stingray, and Turtle to help Eel push heaven higher. Na Areau sent four women to hold up the four corners of heaven. "Your work is done," Na Areau told Eel and struck off his brother's legs. Eel's belly became the Milky Way. His legs fell into the sea and became the eels that swim there today.

Although he had done as his father and grandfather asked, Na Areau the Younger felt he had failed because everything was dark. No one could see his work. He asked his father, Na Atibu, what to do. "Do what you think best," his father replied. So Na Areau the Younger killed his father and used him to give the world light. He flung Na Atibu's right eye into the eastern sky to make the sun. He threw Na Atibu's left eye into the western sky to make the moon. He spread Na Atibu's brain over the heavens to make the stars. He cut his father's flesh into bits to make stones and sand.

Next, Na Areau got his brother Octopus to drag together the stones and sand and got his brother Wave to wash over them so they stuck together. The sand and stones rose above the sea to make a great land, called Samoa. Finally, Na Areau the Younger planted his father's bones to make the first trees.

The World of
THE GILBERT ISLANDS

The Gilbert Islands are a group of 16 small *atolls* (coral reefs) in the central Pacific Ocean, halfway between Australia and Hawaii. They form part of the island country of Kiribati (KIHR uh BAS). The islands are believed to have been inhabited when Samoans settled there between the 1000's and the 1300's.

The myth of Na Areau ➥ the Younger explains the creation of the Milky Way (right) from the belly of Riiki (ree ee kee) the Eel. Many peoples told myths to explain the origin of this band of stars across the night sky. For the Māori (MOW ree) of New Zealand, the Milky Way was the canoe of the warrior hero Tamarereti, who made the stars by throwing shiny pebbles into the sky.

PACIFIC ISLANDS

The Gilbert Islands are an *archipelago* (group of islands) in the South Pacific Ocean. They belong to a larger region known as Micronesia, which includes thousands of islands. The islands of Micronesia and of neighboring Polynesia and Melanesia share many elements of their culture. Their myths often resemble each other. They feature subjects that the islanders would have been familiar with, such as traveling on the ocean or fishing for food.

Many stories across Micronesia involve animals. Many animal characters are tricksters, that can be both helpful and mischievous. In Micronesia the stories often involve the land crab (top) and the turtle or octopus (above); the trickster is usually the rat. On many islands, a fake rat is used as bait for the octopus because they are enemies.

In many mythologies around the world, the sun is represented as being male and the moon female. In Oceania and the Pacific, however, this is often the other way around: The moon is male and the sun is female. They are often thought of as being brother and sister. The moon is male because it allows men to go hunting at night, while the sun allows women to do their work during the day.

LAUFAKANAA

The first Tongans told this myth to explain the origins of the island of 'Ata—also known as Pylstaart Island—and how humanity was created there. The story also explains how humans learned such essential skills as fishing and navigation.

One day, Tamapoulialamafoa (tah mah poh oo lee ah lah mah foh ah), the great Sky God, called together his sons. They were the gods Tangaloa Eiki (tahn gah LOH ah ay ee kee), Tangaloa Tufunga (tahn gah LOH ah too FOONG ah), and Tangaloa Atulongolongo (tahn gah LOH ah ah too lohng oh lohng oh). As Tamapoulialamafoa sat carving wood, he said to them, "Look, my sons. I will shake these wooden shavings, mix them with water, and send them down to Earth." He then told one of his sons to turn into a plover, the bird of the ocean shore, and fly down and see what was happening on Earth. Each day, his son reported back to his father that nothing was happening. Earth was just the same

Finally, one day the son came back and said the shavings had turned into a lovely island, named 'Ata (ah tah). Next, Tamapoulialamafoa sent down a seed, and it turned into a beautiful vine that soon covered the island. The plover pecked at the root until it split in two. Then the root rotted.

The god reported this all to his father, who said, "Fly back again and see what has happened where the root rotted." The plover returned to the island to find a big, juicy worm in the rotted root. He pecked at it and out of the top half came a man called Kohai (koh HAH ee) and out of the bottom half came a man called Kuau (koo AH oo). Then the plover felt something in his beak. It was a tiny bit of worm, which turned into a woman called Momo (moh moh).

So 'Ata became the first island inhabited by humans. The humans needed someone to rule over them, so the great Sky God sent down the god Laufakanaa (lah oo fah kah nah ah) to be their ruler.

Lau means *to speak* and fakanna means *to silence.* Not only was he to rule over 'Ata, he would also be the master of the winds. The gods told him, "Now, Laufakanaa, go below to Earth. You will be in charge of 'Ata, and you can do with it as you please. But you must make wind. If a vessel is caught in stormy winds, and the people beg you to help, you must give them favorable winds so that they and their vessel reach safe harbor. Never create a bad wind that might harm a vessel. Do you understand?" Laufakanaa replied that he did.

So Laufakanaa went down from the sky to 'Ata. There, he made sure that the wind was always favorable. In exchange, the sailors offered him loaves of the bread that they made with oil from grated coconut.

Laufakanaa had taken his fishing net with him to Earth. He caught so many fish that all the people on 'Ata wanted the same net. Finally, Laufakanaa brought with him the banana. He planted it on 'Ata, and before long, banana trees were growing all over the island. Soon the banana seed scattered over neighboring islands, but it first appeared on 'Ata, and it originally came from the sky.

The god also brought a plant called si with him from heaven. A very good root, it can be used to make many different foods to delight the Tongan people. Laufakanaa's kindness did not stop there. He finally planted yam on 'Ata. Then some of the other gods created different kinds of food plants. All of these foods grew on 'Ata before they grew anywhere else in the world.

The World of
THE TONGANS

Tonga comprises about 150 islands in three major groups: Tongatapu, Ha'apai, and Vava'u. Most of the islands in these groups are ring-shaped coral reefs called atolls. Most of Tonga's people live on these islands. A chain of higher, volcanic islands lies west of the coral islands.

The island of 'Ata lies 100 miles (160 kilometers) south of Tongatapu, the main island of the Kingdom of Tonga. Like most of Tonga's islands, 'Ata is now uninhabited. In 1863, many of the people living on the island were kidnapped and sold into slavery. The king of Tonga moved the rest of the islanders to keep them safe.

PRESERVING MYTH

Pacific Islander myths contained important lessons to help peoples relate to the environment in which they lived. They contained information about the sea, the animals who lived on the islands, or aspects of craftwork. On many islands, some men and women had the duty of passing on this knowledge to a younger generation. Fathers passed myths on to their sons, or tribal chiefs or elders passed the stories on to younger people.

The Tongan creator god Tangaloa (tahn gah LOH ah) is more commonly known in Polynesia as Tangaroa (tahn guh RAW ah). This statue of Tangaloa was carved from wood by Polynesians in the 1700's. It probably shows the god creating the other Polynesian gods, and possibly also one of the first men.

FISHING

The importance of fishing in Tongan society is clear in the island's creation myths. In the story of Laufakanaa (lah oo fah kah nah ah), the god teaches the people to fish. Modern Tongans use nets of a similar design. Other Tongan legends tell how the Polynesian gods Maui (MAH oo ee) and Tangaloa created the Tongan islands by pulling them out of the sea using a giant fishhook. Many of Tonga's larger islands are covered with fertile soil, and agriculture is the main source of income. But for most Tongans, the sea is their main source of food.

Men and a woman sail along the coast of what is now a Tongan island in outrigger boats, in an illustration made during Captain James Cook's final voyage to the Pacific Ocean in the late 1770's. A common boat in the Pacific Islands, an outrigger has a float, a long log that runs parallel to the boat and is linked to it by a frame. The float acts as a counterbalance, or secondary hull, to prevent the boat from tipping over.

The Jealous Sun and His

The people of Papua New Guinea have traditionally used this myth to explain why the sun is sometimes almost unbearably hot.

A long time ago, a brave hunter called Aruako (ah roo AH koh) could not find a girl he liked well enough to marry. One day, while he was walking in the forest, he discovered what he thought was a beautiful girl, alone, bathing in a pond. (In fact, she was really the spirit of the moon.)

"I remember you," she said, "you dug me like a root from Mother Earth." And, indeed, Aruako had. A number of years before, he had dug a beautiful white disc from the earth. The white disc had grown brighter and brighter in his arms. It finally grew so large that Aruako could not hold it, and it had drifted away from him. "I can see that you have fallen in love with me," continued the beautiful woman, "but it can never be. I am a spirit and you are a human, and I am promised to the sun."

But Aruako could not stop staring at her. "Listen," he said, "I unearthed you and set you free. You must surely belong to me." He took her by the hand and led her through the forest. At first, she was reluctant to go, but he was so kind that she followed him. They spent the night in his house deep in the forest, and everything was calm and peaceful. In the sky, the stars twinkled in a gentle breeze.

Beloved Moon

When Aruako awoke the next morning, the moon spirit was gone. He searched high and low, but he could not find her. Meanwhile, the sun grew higher in the sky, pouring its fury on Aruako. He grew so hot that he fainted. When he woke up, he crawled to his village, barely able to breathe. The rays of the sun beat down on him like a hammer.

Two boys found Aruako collapsed upon a path in the village. The villagers went to his aid. "Maybe he has been bitten by a snake, or perhaps it is sun sickness," said one. They put cold cloths on his face to cool him, but he was too sick to eat or drink. Aruako's family sat by his bedside, fanning him with palm fronds, but the sunlight pushed past the palm-leaf fans and burned Aruako. His skin blistered; his tears dried up; and his tongue swelled and filled his mouth.

"Feel him," said Aruako's mother to his sisters. "The sun is killing him. Look how it has destroyed all the shade." Aruako grew weaker and weaker. Finally, the sun sank below the horizon, and the lovely moon appeared. But it was too late for Aruako, who died. Today, the people of the village turn their faces from the moon, afraid that if they stare at her for too long, the sun will get jealous and burn them with his heat.

The World of THE PAPUANS

Papua New Guinea is an independent nation in the Pacific Ocean, north of Australia. It consists of part of the island of New Guinea plus a chain of tropical islands that extends more than 1,000 miles (1,600 kilometers).

The people of Papua New Guinea speak more than 700 languages related to particular ethnic groups. Most peoples of the Pacific Islands speak languages that belong to a group known as the Austronesian family. The languages on New Guinea do not belong to this family. They developed earlier and differently. The most important second language on Papua New Guinea is Pidgin, which is the island's *lingua franca* (common language). About 65 to 70 percent of the words in Pidgin are derived from English. Another 25 to 30 percent of the words come from local languages, of which Tolai is the most important. About 5 percent of the words come from the German language. There are also a few Malay and Portuguese words.

Wooden statues stand outside a spirit house in Papua New Guinea. The spirit house, traditionally forbidden to all but initiated warriors, is the most important building in a village.

SKY AND LAND

Papuans have traditionally believed that the sky and the land are so closely linked that they are parts of the same world. They believe that a sky spirit slid down to Earth on a rope to go fishing. But when he wanted to return to the sky, he discovered that the rope had been cut. He was trapped on Earth! The sky spirit cried so loudly that his wife threw down four cucumbers for him to eat. The four cucumbers turned into new wives. The Papuans believe they are the children of that sky spirit and his new wives.

MAGIC MASKS

Some Papuan masks have a spiritual meaning. Some masks are worn for ritual dances. Other masks represent dead ancestors or the spirits who protect the tribe. These masks are hung in homes rather than worn.

The people of Papua New Guinea are expert farmers. People in the highlands of what is now the island of New Guinea may have been the first to domesticate yams and taro around 7000 B.C. (A starchy portion of the stem of the yam and of taro grows underground and is edible. This portion is called a tuber in yams and a corm in taro.) The people of New Guinea may also have been the first to domesticate bananas and sugar cane.

Papua New Guinea is one of the most rural countries in the world. Less than 20 percent of its population live in towns and cities. The rest live in traditional communities on the New Guinea mainland and dozens of islands in the Melanesia Archipelago.

In the highlands of Papua New Guinea, people still use pigments to decorate their bodies for festivals and ceremonies. The designs are related to their clan, so body-decorating helps to reinforce an individual's identity as a member of a social group.

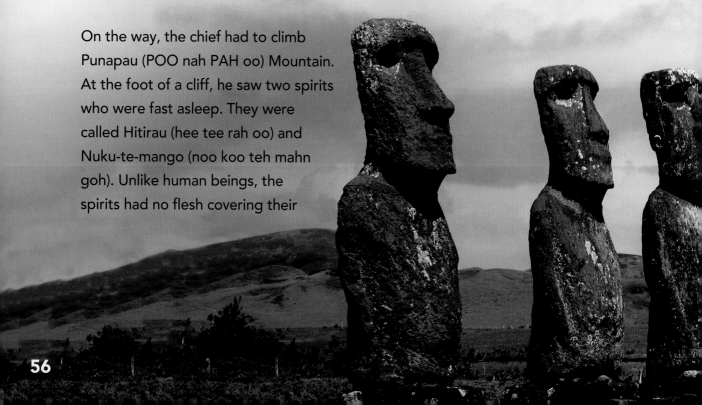

THE WOODEN MOAI

The Easter Islanders told this myth to explain the origins of the wooden figures that the men of the island wore around their necks on special occasions.

Chief Tu-uko-ihu (too oo koh ee hoo) was the first chief of the island known as Rapa Nui (RAH puh NOO ee). One day, he decided to cross the island to his second house, which was at a place called Ahu Hanga Hahave. He left early in the morning so he would have enough time to reach the house before nightfall.

On the way, the chief had to climb Punapau (POO nah PAH oo) Mountain. At the foot of a cliff, he saw two spirits who were fast asleep. They were called Hitirau (hee tee rah oo) and Nuku-te-mango (noo koo teh mahn goh). Unlike human beings, the spirits had no flesh covering their

bodies, and the chief could see their ribs and hollow bellies.

The chief hurried past the two spirits. He knew that if the spirits realized that he had seen them—a sight forbidden to humans—they would have him killed. But another spirit woke up Hitirau and Nuku-te-mango, saying, "Wake up, the chief has seen our naked ribs." When the two spirits looked up, all they could see was the back of the chief as he climbed the mountain. They ran after him, and when they had caught up with him, they demanded to know exactly what he had seen. "Nothing," replied Chief Tu-uko-ihu. The spirits did not believe him and asked him again, "Chief, are you sure that you saw nothing?" "I saw nothing," the chief replied again. The spirits asked him three more times what he had seen; each time, he said he had seen nothing.

When Chief Tu-uko-ihu arrived at Ahu Hanga Hahave, the two spirits made themselves invisible and floated around the house. They waited for the chief to tell the other humans what he had seen on his walk over. But he said nothing. At that time, the people of the village were opening the ovens in which they had cooked their food. After retrieving their food, they threw out the end pieces of burning wood. Chief Tu-uko-ihu picked up two of these pieces and took them to his house. Using a sharp piece of a beautiful black rock, he carved the wood into two figures to represent the two spirits, Hitirau and Nuku-te-mango, with their ribs sticking out. He called these carvings moai kavakava (MOH eye kah vah kah vah). When he finished carving them, he fell asleep. He dreamed of two women spirits. When he woke up, he carved them exactly as they had appeared to him in his dream. He called these carvings of women spirits moai paepae (moh AH ee pah eh pah eh).

The news spread about the wooden carvings. Everyone wanted one. Some people gave Tu-uko-ihu something in exchange, such as seabirds, fish, and yams, but others wanted carvings for nothing. One evening, Tu-uko-ihu told those greedy people to follow him. They went into his house and saw the moai dancing on their own. They were so frightened that that they quickly offered the chief food for the carvings. From that day on, the house was known as the House of Walking Images.

The World of
RAPA NUI

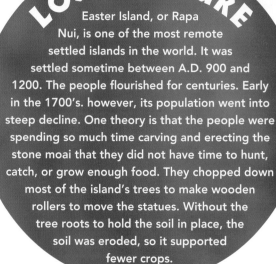

Easter Island in the South Pacific Ocean is famous as the site of enormous statues of people that were carved hundreds of years ago. The island, which is also known by its Polynesian name Rapa Nui (RAH puh NOO ee), lies about 2,300 miles (3,700 kilometers) west of Chile.

This myth tells how Chief Tu-uko-ihu (too oo koh ee hoo) carved the first wooden statues on Rapa Nui, now known as Easter Island. The statues, known as moai kavakava (MOH eye kah vah kah vah), were carved with pieces of obsidian (ob SIHD ee uhn), black volcanic rock that can be given a sharp edge, and later with knives. The figures appeared as emaciated and half-decayed bodies, with ribs that stuck out, because this was how the Easter Islanders pictured the spirits of the dead. The islanders chanted to the carvings and danced with them, which suggests they were used for religious ceremonies.

LOST CULTURE

Easter Island, or Rapa Nui, is one of the most remote settled islands in the world. It was settled sometime between A.D. 900 and 1200. The people flourished for centuries. Early in the 1700's. however, its population went into steep decline. One theory is that the people were spending so much time carving and erecting the stone moai that they did not have time to hunt, catch, or grow enough food. They chopped down most of the island's trees to make wooden rollers to move the statues. Without the tree roots to hold the soil in place, the soil was eroded, so it supported fewer crops.

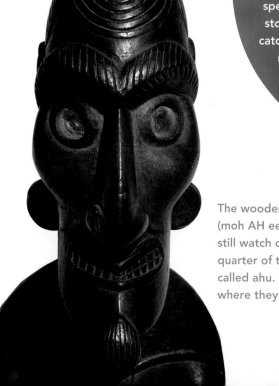

The wooden carvings described in "The Wooden Maoi (moh AH ee)" have their stone equivalent in the moai that still watch over the landscape on Rapa Nui. Only about one quarter of the statues were erected on stone platforms called ahu. Over half of the statues never left the quarry where they were carved.

58

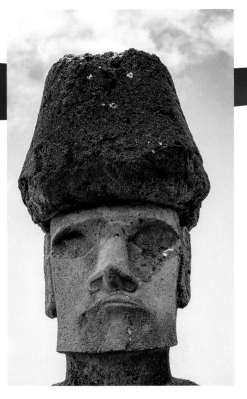

Moai in Rapa Nui National Park stand with their backs to the ocean and their faces looking over the island. The statues were possibly intended to honor ancestors. Today, more than 600 statues are scattered on the island. Most are from 11 to 20 feet (3.4 to 6 meters) tall. Some weigh as much as 90 tons (82 metric tons). The islanders used stone hand picks to carve the statues from the rock of an extinct volcano.

A few stone moai wear "hats" of a light red rock named scoria. The headgear, known as pukao, probably gave a statue increased importance. Throughout the Pacific, red is considered a sacred color.

Actors in the 1994 film *Rapa Nui* move a giant moai across the island using muscle power and ropes. How the huge statues were taken the 11 miles (18 kilometers) from the quarry where most of them were carved to their final standing position has long puzzled scientists because the islanders had no wheels or cranes or animals to pull the stones. The filmmakers presented one theory proposed by scientists: The large-bellied moai were tilted forward and then moved by rocking them from side to side.

DEITIES OF AUSTRALIA, NEW ZEALAND, AND PACIFIC ISLANDS

Alinga (uh leen guh)
According to the Aboriginal peoples of Australia, Alinga the Lizard Man was a famous hunter whose favorite boomerang created Uluru.

Baiame (by uh mee)
In what is now the Australian state of New South Wales, Aboriginal peoples told stories about their great ancestor, Baiame. He was an ancient sky god who created all things and taught people useful skills.

Haumia (huh oo mee uh)
Among the Māori of New Zealand, Haumia is the god of wild food.

Kunmanggur (koon MAHNG gur)
Kunmanggur is the name the Murinbata people of Australia use for the Rainbow Snake, who appears in the myths of other Aboriginal peoples under different names. In the Dreamtime, Rainbow Snake left the waterholes where he lived and created the features of the Australian outback with his body.

Laufakanaa (lah oo fah kah nah ah)
In Tonga, Laufakanaa is the god of the winds. He was sent to Earth by the sky god in order to rule the island of 'Ata and to ensure that sailors had fair winds. Laufakanaa brought such plants from heaven as the banana, which became one of the Tongans' major foods, and he taught the people how to fish.

Marmoo (mahr moo)
For the Aboriginal people in what is today the Australian state of New South Wales, Marmoo was the god of evil, who attempted to undo all the good done by the creator god Baiame.

Maui (MAH oo ee)
Maui was a popular trickster god who features in many stories throughout Polynesia. Some of the most common myths about the tiny Maui told how he fished up islands from the bottom of the sea and how he stole fire to help humankind.

Na Areau (nah ahr ee oo)
In the Gilbert Islands of Polynesia, Na Areau, the "spider lord," was the creator of all things. Among his descendants was Na Areau the Younger, who was an important trickster god.

Na Atibu (nah ah tee boo)
One of the first beings created by the Polynesian god Na Areau, Na Atibu helped his father create the world. He allowed his son, Na Areau the Younger, to slay him in order to create light.

Papa (pah pah)
To the Māori of New Zealand, Papa was the Earth mother; she had to be separated from her husband, Rangi, the sky god, to make room for the Earth to be created.

Papa (pah pah)

In Hawaii, Papa is seen as the Earth goddess and mother of all the gods. She is also said to be the ancestress of the Hawaiian people.

Pele (PEH leh)

The Polynesians told how the beautiful fire goddess Pele wandered widely before she settled on Hawaii. Since her sister, Hi'iaka, stole Pele's lover, Lohiau, Pele has been infamous for the outbursts of temper that cause lava to spill out from Hawaii's volcanoes.

Rangi (RAHN gee)

The Māori of New Zealand saw Rangi as the sky father, who with his wife, Papa, brought the world into being.

Rongo (raw ngaw)

Among the Māori of New Zealand, Rongo is the god of cultivated food, such as taro and kumara.

Tāne (TUH neh)

Tāne, or Tāne-mahuta, was the Māori god of the forests and everything that lives in them. He played a key role in separating his parents, Rangi and Papa, to allow the world to come into being.

Tangaloa (tahn gah LOH ah)

In Tongan mythology, the Tangaloa were an important family of deities descended from Lord Tangaloa, the sky god.

Tangaroa (tahn guh RAW ah)

Among the Polynesians, Tangaroa was the god of fish and reptiles. He was an important deity for a people that live on islands surrounded by water.

Tāwhiri (tah HWEE ree)

The Māori of New Zealand see Tāwhiri, or Tāwhirimātea, as the god of weather, and especially of storms. In Māori mytholoy, Tāwhiri disagreed with his brothers' decision to separate their parents, Papa and Rangi. Tāwhiri fought against his brothers, destroying the forests of Tāne, driving Tangaroa into the sea, and becoming an eternal enemy of the war god, Tū.

Tjinimin (chihn IHM ihn)

The Murinbata Aborigines of Australia viewed Tjinimin as a trickster spirit who tried to kill his father, Kunmanggur, the Rainbow Snake.

Tūmatauenga (too mah tah oo EHN gah)

For the Māori of New Zealand, Tu or Tūmatauenga was one of the most important gods among the children of Rangi and Papa. He was the god of war, and warriors prayed to him before battle. Because Tu defeated his brothers, humans may now also harness the resources the other gods control, including wild and cultivated crops.

GLOSSARY

archipelago A large number of islands grouped closely together.

atoll A ring-shaped island formed from coral.

constellation A group of stars that form an identifiable pattern, such as an animal or a mythological figure.

coral A hard, stony substance created by millions of tiny marine animals that form reefs or islands.

creation The process by which the universe was brought into being.

creator In myth, a creator god is one that creates the universe or the earth, geographical features, and often all humans or a particular culture. Creation myths explain the origins of the world, but often do so by describing actions that seem to take place in a world that already exists.

cult A system of religious devotion based on a particular individual or object.

Dreamtime The creation as understood by Aboriginal peoples in Australia, when the world was created by sacred ancestors whose spirits remain in the world.

evacuated Moved from a place of danger to somewhere safe.

Micronesia A subregion of Oceania that includes thousands of small islands in the western Pacific Ocean.

moai A carved statue from Rapa Nui (Easter Island), especially the giant stone heads for which the island is famous.

myth A traditional story that a people tell to explain their own origins or the origins of natural and social phenomena. Myths often involve gods, spirits, and other supernatural beings.

phenomena Things that can be observed or seen to be real.

Polynesia A subregion of Oceania in the central and southern Pacific Ocean that includes more than 1,000 islands.

reef A ridge of rock or coral just beneath the surface of the sea.

ritual A solemn religious ceremony in which a set of actions are performed in a specific order.

sacred Something that is connected with the gods or goddesses and so should be treated with respectful worship.

sacrifice An offering made to a god or gods, often in the form of an animal or even a person who is killed for the purpose. Sacrifices also take the shape of valued possessions that might be buried, placed in caves, or thrown into a lake for the gods.

Songline A route through the Australian landscape that the spirits traveled during the Dreamtime, and the songs or stories that record the journey.

supernatural Describes something that cannot be explained by science or by the laws of nature, which is therefore said to be caused by beings such as gods, spirits, or ghosts.

tattoo A permanent design created by inserting ink or other pigment into the skin through puncture holes.

trickster A supernatural figure who engages in mischievous activities that either benefit or harm humans. The motives behind a trickster's behavior are not always clear. Tricksters appear in various shapes in myths around the world, including Maui in Polynesian and Coyote and Raven in Native American cultures.

FOR FURTHER INFORMATION

Books

Andersen, Johannes C. *Myths and Legends of the Polynesians*. Dover Publications Ltd, 1995.

Children's Book of Mythical Beasts & Magical Monsters. DK Publishing, 2011.

Craig, Robert D. *Handbook of Polynesian Mythology* (World Mythology.) ABC-CLIO, 2004.

Dalal, Anita. *Myths of Oceania* (Mythic World). Raintree Steck Vaughn, 2002.

Hulley, Charles E. *The Rainbow Serpent*. New Holland, 2000.

Marshall, James Vance. *Stories from the Billabong*. Frances Lincoln Children's Books, 2008.

Mills, Alice. *New World Mythology: Myths and Legends of Oceania and the Americas*. Global Book Publishing, 2009.

National Geographic Essential Visual History of World Mythology. National Geographic Society, 2008.

Orbell, Margaret. *The Illustrated Encyclopedia of Māori Myth and Legend*. Canterbury University Press, 1995.

Philip, Neil. *Eyewitness Mythology* (DK Eyewitness Books). DK Publishing, 2011.

Reed, A. W. *Aboriginal Myths: Tales of the Dreamtime*. New Holland, 2006.

Reed, A. W. *Māori Myth and Legend*. Raupo Publishing Ltd, 2011.

Reed, A. W. *Myths and Legends of Polynesia*. Reed Publishing, 1974.

Smith, W. Ramsay. *Myths and Legends of the Australian Aborigines*. Dover Publications, 2003.

Te Kanawa, Kiri. *Land of the Long White Cloud: Māori Myths, Tales and Legends*. Arcade Publishing, 1989.

Websites

http://saleonard.people.ysu.edu/oceanaother.html
Scott Leonard's page of links to resources about myths of Oceania.

http://www.godchecker.com/pantheon/australian-mythology.php
A directory of Australian deities from God Checker, written in a light-hearted style but with accurate information.

http://www.godchecker.com/pantheon/oceanic-mythology.php
The God Checker index of Oceanic deities, with links to individual entries.

http://www.pantheon.org/areas/mythology/oceania/polynesian
Encyclopedia Mythica page with links to many pages about myths from Polynesian and Hawaiian cultures.

http://www.pantheon.org/areas/mythology/oceania/aboriginal
Encyclopedia Mythica page with links to pages about Australian myths.

http://www.mythome.org/culturl.html
The Myth Home directory of myths by culture features links to "Austro-Zealander," "Hawaiian," and "South Seas" myths.

http://www.sacred-texts.com/pac/index.htm
Sacred Texts has a directory of myths from Polynesia.

http://www.sacred-texts.com/aus/index.htm
Sacred Texts directory of Australian myths.

INDEX

PRONUNCIATION KEY

Sound	As in
a	hat, map
ah	father, far
ai	care, air
aw	order
aw	all
ay	age, face
ch	child, much
ee	equal, see
ee	machine, city
eh	let, best
ih	it, pin, hymn
k	coat, look
o	hot, rock
oh	open, go
oh	grow, tableau
oo	rule, move, food
ow	house, out
oy	oil, voice
s	say, nice
sh	she, abolition
u	full, put
u	wood
uh	cup, butter
uh	flood
uh	about, ameba
uh	taken, purple
uh	pencil
uh	lemon
uh	circus
uh	labyrinth
uh	curtain
uh	Egyptian
uh	section
uh	fabulous
ur	term, learn, sir, work
y	icon, ice, five
yoo	music
zh	pleasure